Nelson Handwriting

Pupil Book 1A

D1614606

OXFORD
UNIVERSITY PRESS

OXFORD
UNIVERSITY PRESS

Great Clarendon Street, Oxford, OX2 6DP, United Kingdom

Oxford University Press is a department of the University of Oxford.
It furthers the University's objective of excellence in research, scholarship,
and education by publishing worldwide. Oxford is a registered trade mark
of Oxford University Press in the UK and in certain other countries

Nelson Handwriting previous edition first published by Nelson Thornes Ltd in 2003

This edition published by Oxford University Press in 2016

British Library Cataloguing in Publication Data

Data available

ISBN: 978-0-19-836852-6

12

Paper used in the production of this book is a natural, recyclable product made from
wood grown in sustainable forests. The manufacturing process conforms to the
environmental regulations of the country of origin.

Printed in China by Golden Cup

Acknowledgements

Cover illustration: Magali Morales
Cover flap illustration: Nigel Kitching

Page make-up: OKS Prepress, India

Acknowledgement has been made to Alexander Inglis as the
original developer of the Nelson Handwriting script.

Oxford OWL
Discover eBooks, inspirational
resources, advice and support
www.oxfordowl.co.uk

Contents

C

as cool as a cat

Focus

A Look at these letters.

c o a d g f s q e

B Copy these letters into your book.

ccc   ooo   aaa

ddd   ggg   fff

sss   qqq   eee

Remember,
all letters
start at the
top, except,
d and e.

Introducing letter families: Set 1 (c o a d g f s q e)

Copy these words into your book.
Take care to form your letters correctly.

cod   dog   fog

sad   sag   gas

> Remember, the letters d and f are almost twice the height of a small letter, like a.

Extension

Look at the words in the box below.

fog   dog

Complete these sentences in your book.
Write in the missing words.

1 My ____ likes a walk.

2 I walked in the ____.

UNIT 2

d

a good dog

Focus

A Copy this pattern into your book.

cccc cccc cccc

B Copy these letters into your book.

co   co   co   co   co

ad   ad   ad   ad   ad

gs   gs   gs   gs   gs

qe   qe   qe   qe   qe

> Remember, the letters g and q are descenders. Their tails go below the line.

Practising letter families: Set 1 (c o g d a f s q e

Make these words. Copy them into your book.

d + ad = dad dad dad

s + ad = sad sad sad

f + ad = fad fad fad

> Take care!
> The letter f is a tall letter. Its tail also goes below the line.

Complete this caption in your book, using two words from the box below.

sad had dad fad lad

_____ is _____

lemon jelly

Focus

A Look at these letters.

i l t j u y

B Copy these letters into your book.

iii lll ttt

jjj uuu yyy

Introducing letter families: Set 2 (i l t j u y)

Copy these words into your book.

ill   ill   ill   ill

pill pill pill pill

Remember, the letter l is an ascender. It is a tall letter.

Extension

Look at the words in the box below.

pill   ill

Complete these sentences in your book.
Write in the missing words.

1 Jill was _____.

2 A _____ made her better.

I am little.

Focus

A Copy this pattern into your book.

ʋʋʋ   ʋʋʋ   ʋʋʋ   ʋʋʋ

B Copy these letters into your book.

it   it   it   it   it

tl   tl   tl   tl   tl

uy   uy   uy   uy   uy

jy   jy   jy   jy   jy

> Remember, the letter t is not quite as tall as an ascender.

Practising letter families: Set 2 (i l t j u y)

Extra

Copy these words into your book.

little little little little

lolly lolly lolly lolly

Take care! The letter i is the same height as a small letter, like e.

Extension

Copy this sentence into your book.

Lucy has a little lolly.

Park fun!

A Look at these letters.

b h k m n p r

Copy this pattern into your book.

nnnn nnnn nnnn

B Copy these letters into your book.

rrr   nnn mmm
hhh bbb kkk ppp

Introducing letter families: Set 3 (b h k m n p r)

Copy these words into your book.

an   ran   nan   man

ark hark bark park

> Remember the letters h, b and k are ascenders. They are the same height as capital letters.

Copy these sentences into your book.

1 Nan had a run.

2 Nan has fun in the park.

What is in the sink?

A Copy this pattern into your book.

nlnl nlnl nlnl nlnl

B Copy these letters into your book.

nk   nk   nk   nk   nk

rp   rp   rp   rp   rp

nm   nm   nm   nm   nm

bh   bh   bh   bh   bh

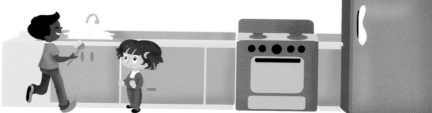

Practising letter families: Set 3 (b h k m n p r)

Make these words. Copy them into your book.

pi + nk = pink pink pink

bu + nk = bunk bunk bunk

Extension

Choose the right word from the boxes to fill the gaps.
Copy and complete the sentences in your book.

1   sink   Jenny put her _____ pens
    pink   in her bag.

2   sunk   Sita had the top _____.
    bunk

The bees buzzed.

Focus

A Look at these letters.

V   W   X   Z

B Copy these letters into your book.

VVVVV   WWWWW

XXXXX   ZZZZZ

Introducing letter families: Set 4 (v w x z)

Copy these words into your book.

x-ray   x-ray   x-ray

zoo   zoo   zoo

was   was   was

very   very   very

Look at the words in the box below.

was   very   x-ray   zoo

Copy these sentences into your book.
Write in the missing words.

1 We saw a ____ big
zebra at the ____.

2 He ____ having an ____.

Will waved at the zebra.

Focus

A Copy this pattern into your book.

WWW WWW WWW WWW

B Copy these letters into your book.

VW   VW   VW   VW   VW

XW   XW   XW   XW   XW

XZ   XZ   XZ   XZ   XZ

ZZ   ZZ   ZZ   ZZ   ZZ

Practising letter families: Set 4 (v w x z)

Choose w or z to complete the words below.
Write the words into your book.

_oo   _ebra   bu_ _

_as   _asp   _ent

Copy this sentence into your book.

Zoe went to the vet.

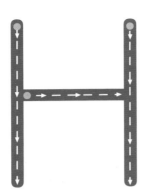

I can go Here or There.

Focus

A Copy this pattern into your book.

B Write these capital letters three times in your book.

E F H I T L

Remember, capital letters are the same height as ascenders.

Practising capital letters

Look at the children and the places they visited on holiday.
Match the children and the places that begin with the same letter.
Write each pair in your book.

Freya, Isabella, Luke

Italy, France, London

Extension

Use each pair of words from **Extra** to make a sentence in your book.
An example has been done for you.

Tim went to Turkey.

I have read from A to Z.

Focus

A Copy this pattern into your book.

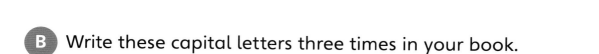

B Write these capital letters three times in your book.

A K M N V W X Y Z

> Remember, capital letters start at the top when you write them.

Copy these sentences into your book.
Complete each one by writing an activity you do.

1 On Monday I _____ .

2 On Tuesday I _____ .

Extension

Look at the days of the week.
Copy them into your book in the correct order.

Tuesday

Friday

Monday

Wednesday

Thursday

A year goes from January
to December.

Focus

A Copy this pattern into your book.

B Write these capital letters three times in your book.

B D C G O Q S P R U J

Practising capital letters

Look at the words in the box below.

February   January

Copy these sentences into your book.
Complete each one by choosing the
correct month of the year.

1 The first month of the year

is _____.

2 The next month is _____.

Extension

Look at the first six months of the year.
Copy them into your book in the correct order.

June   May

January   March

February   April

I was 5, now I am 6!

Focus

Look at these numbers.
Copy each number three times into your book.

1 2 3 4 5 6 7 8 9 10

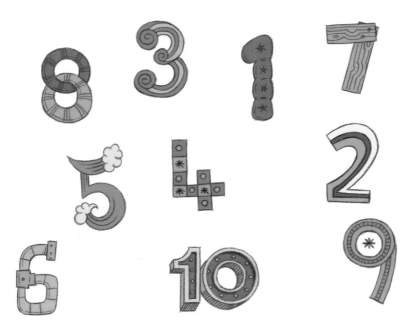

> Remember, numbers begin at the top when you write them.

Copy these sentences into your book.
Write the correct number to complete each sentence.

1 There are ___ days in a week.

2 There are ___ months in a year.

3 I am ___ years old.

Copy the sentences above into your book,
using the words instead of the numerals.
The first one has been done for you.

There are <u>**seven**</u> days in a week.

p b g
j q z x

A big ape jumped on the stage.

Focus

Copy these letters into your book.

age   age   age   age   age

ape   ape   ape   ape   ape

aze   aze   aze   aze   aze

Make these words. Copy them into your book.

tap + e = tape   tape   tape

cub + e = cube   cube   cube

pip + e = pipe   pipe   pipe

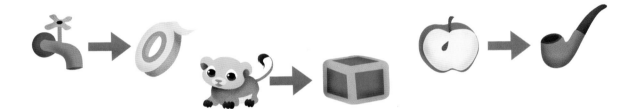

Choose age or aze to complete these words.
Copy them into your book.

1 p_____

2 st_____

3 m_____

4 abl_____

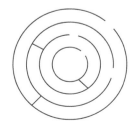

un

Please unlock the gate.

A Copy this pattern into your book.

UUl UUl UUl UUl

B Copy these letters into your book.

un un un un un

um um um um um

ur ur ur ur ur

Practising consistent size and height of small letters

Make these words. Copy them into your book.

un + load = unload   unload

un + pack = unpack   unpack

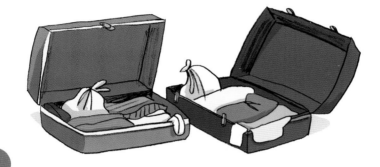

Extension

Copy these sentences into your book.

1 Let's unload the car.

2 Then we can unpack the picnic.

Focus

Copy these patterns into your book.

cccc cccc cccc cccc

nnnn nnnn nnnn nnnn

Extra

Copy these words into your book.

dog   sad   fill   lift

bin   park   vow   zip

Extension

Copy this sentence into your book.

Jack and Jill went up the hill.